God Made You, And He Does Not Make Junk

Discovering the You That God Had in Mind

Cindy H. Carr, D.Min, MACL

This book is published by CHC Connect.

Printed in the United States of America
First Edition, 2025

ISBN: 978-1-971192-02-4

For permissions or inquiries, contact:
Cindy H. Carr
cindyhcarr@outlook.com
www.cindyhcarr.com

Acknowledgements

To all those who have allowed me the privilege of walking beside you on your journey—this book is dedicated to you.

I cannot name you individually, for you are too many, and each of your stories too sacred. But you have profoundly shaped my life. You taught me far more than I ever taught you. Your courage, your honesty, your vulnerability, and your willingness to let me see into the deepest parts of your story have left an imprint on me that is immeasurable.

It was through your journeys that I came to know more of God—His compassion, His creativity, His tenderness, and His healing power. And it is because of what I learned from walking with you that I am able to hold space for others with greater grace, understanding, and hope.

Thank you for trusting me.
Thank you for teaching me.
Thank you for allowing your story to shape mine.

This book exists because of you.

Table of Contents

How to Use This Book 6

Preface 7

Introduction 9

Chapter 1
In His Image: The Foundation of Identity............... 14

Chapter 2
God Saw It Was Good: Living From Blessing,
Not Brokenness 20

Chapter 3
Fearfully and Wonderfully Made.............................. 27

Chapter 4
Known Before Birth.. 34

Chapter 5
Called Through Weakness... 40

Chapter 6
Positioned for Purpose.. 46

Chapter 7
Shaped in Hidden Places... 53

Chapter 8
Shaped Through Adversity.. 59

Chapter 9
You Are God's Workmanship.................................... 65

Chapter 10
One Body, Many Members....................................... 71

Chapter 11
Grace to Speak, Grace to Serve................................. 77

Chapter 12
The Greatest of These Is Love.................................... 83

Chapter 13
Your Unique Design.. 90

Chapter 14
Living from Your Design.. 97

Epilogue 103

Appendix A

Crafting Your Design Discovery Declaration 107

About the Author 110

How to Use This Book

1. Read each chapter slowly and prayerfully.

2. Complete the Reflection Questions and Design

> *Discovery Puzzle Pieces at the end of each chapter. Across the book you will collect fourteen puzzle pieces, each one a small but powerful insight into your Design Discovery Declaration at the end.*

3. Transfer all fourteen puzzle pieces to page 108.

4. Use your puzzle pieces to craft your personal Design Discovery Declaration on page 109.

5. Let this declaration guide how you live.

> *Your Design Discovery Declaration becomes a compass for your life—an anchor that helps you recognize alignment and resist striving.*

> *This book is not about becoming someone else. It is about remembering who you already are.*

Preface

For many years in ministry, I have had the privilege of walking alongside people in some of their most vulnerable seasons—seeking identity, struggling with purpose, wrestling with insecurity, or simply wanting to know why their life felt heavier than it should. Again and again, I discovered a pattern: when people began to understand how God uniquely created them, something shifted. When they stopped striving to fix every perceived flaw, stopped chasing promotions of worthiness, and stopped measuring themselves by someone else's strengths, a new kind of freedom emerged.

As we explored their God-given design—natural skills, abilities, callings, wiring, temperament, and talents—I watched people come alive. Not because they became perfect, and not because life suddenly grew easy, but because they finally stepped into alignment with who they truly were. And in that alignment, something sacred happened:
a peace that surpasses all understanding,
and a joy of the Lord that became their strength.

By contrast, those who continued striving—trying to strengthen every weakness, adopting endless self-help strategies, or performing in hopes of acceptance—rarely found sustainable peace. Their lives often filled with pressure instead of purpose, exhaustion instead of joy.

This book was born from that realization.

My hope is that its pages will empower you to discover (or rediscover) how God intentionally created you, and to embrace a way of living that flows from that divine design. You were crafted with purpose. You were shaped with intention. You were made by a God who does not make mistakes—and who certainly does not make junk.

If you can learn to live in agreement with that truth, your life will not simply improve—it will flourish. My prayer is that this book becomes a companion on that journey, helping you step into the peace, joy, and purpose that have been waiting for you all along.

Introduction

Most people move through life carrying an unspoken question:

"Who am I… really?"

We spend years trying to fit into molds, roles, expectations, and identities handed to us by family, culture, trauma, or comparison. We learn to measure ourselves by what we do, what we produce, or how well we perform. And somewhere along the way, we begin to assume that who we really are—beneath the layers—is not quite enough.

But what if the deepest truth about you is not something you achieve, but something you receive?

What if identity is not something you build, but something God already built into you?

What if the story of Scripture is not merely about what God has done in history, but also about who God has created you to be today?

This book is rooted in a simple but life-altering conviction:

God made you. And He doesn't make junk.

Before you ever took your first breath, God imagined you, formed you, shaped you, and designed you with intention. You are not an accident. You are not an afterthought. You are not a mistake God is trying to fix. You are an expression of His creativity, His craftsmanship, and His love.

And yet, if we're honest, most of us don't feel that way.

We feel fragmented.

We feel insecure.

We feel unsure of our gifts, unclear about our calling, and uncertain of our value.

We feel like everyone else understands their place—except us.

But throughout the Bible, we see a God who lovingly, patiently reveals identity to His people. He spoke identity over Adam and Eve before they ever worked the garden. He formed David in the secret places. He knew Jeremiah before he was born. He rewired Paul. He renamed Gideon. He called Esther for a specific moment in time. And He shaped countless "ordinary" people with extraordinary purpose—many of whom never make the spotlight.

Each story whispers the same truth:

God forms people intentionally—and He forms them differently.

This book will walk you through a journey of discovering exactly how God formed you.

Not the version of you shaped by fear.

Not the version shaped by people-pleasing.

Not the version shaped by comparison or disappointment.

But the version God imagined from the beginning.

Through Scripture, reflection, story, and a practical process I call the Design Discovery Journey, we will explore five essential movements of identity:

1. Design — Who God made you

2. Desire — What God writes on your heart

3. Drive — Your internal motivational wiring

4. Gifts — How the Spirit works through you

5. Grace — The unique way your life expresses God to the world

Each chapter includes a "Design Discovery" reflection—small but powerful insights that, by the end of the book, come together in a personalized Design Discovery Declaration. This declaration is not simply a statement you write; it becomes a roadmap for living confidently and authentically as the person God crafted you to be.

You will meet well-known biblical figures—but also lesser-known individuals whose lives, though quieter, carried enormous Kingdom significance. Their stories demonstrate that God does not reserve purpose for the platformed, the famous, or the powerful.

He works through the overlooked, the in-between, the ordinary, and the unexpected.

He works through people like you.

This book is not about self-help.

It is about God-shaped identity.

It is not about discovering your personal potential.

It is about uncovering God's intentional design.

It is not about becoming a "better version" of yourself.

It is about becoming your truest, God-crafted self.

My prayer is that as you read these pages, something awakens inside you—something ancient, something holy, something that has been waiting to be named. And by the time you finish, you will not simply know more about Scripture...

You will know more about yourself, and the God who made you on purpose, with purpose, for purpose.

So take a deep breath.

You are loved.

You are seen.

You were made with intention.

And your journey of Design Discovery begins right now.

Chapter 1

In His Image: The Foundation of Identity

In the opening pages of Scripture, before humanity took a breath, before there were commandments, cultures, or even sin, God made a declaration about who we are. Identity wasn't an afterthought. It wasn't something added once humanity matured or once they proved themselves. It was the very first gift He placed over us. "Let us make mankind in our image, in our likeness." With those words, God established the foundation for every human life. You were created as a reflection of God—not accidentally, not partially, and not conditionally. Before you ever accomplished anything, God decided you would bear His likeness. Your story does not begin with your beginning. It begins with God's desire.

This is the part most people never fully embrace. We are so accustomed to defining ourselves by what we do, what we struggle with, what we've survived, or what others have said about us, that we forget the first and truest thing about us: we were made in the image of God. Identity, then, is not something we achieve. It is something we receive. We don't create it; we uncover it. We don't manufacture it; we learn to accept what God has already said.

And yet, if we're honest, most of us do not move through the world like image-bearers. We walk through life feeling fragmented, insecure, unsure of our gifts, uncertain of our calling, or disconnected from any sense of divine purpose. We feel like we're stumbling into identity rather than living from it. We wonder why knowing who we are feels so complicated, so fragile, so easily shaken.

It's because the first spiritual battle in history was an identity battle. The enemy did not begin by attacking Adam and Eve's morality or productivity. He attacked their trust in God, and therefore their understanding of themselves. "Did God really say…?" was not a question about fruit—it was a question designed to fracture identity. If the enemy can distort how you see God, he will distort how you see yourself. Every lie about God leads to a lie about you.

But God never wavered from His first declaration. When He created humanity, He spoke goodness and blessing over them. They had not accomplished anything, yet God looked at them and said that His creation was very good. That blessing still echoes over your life today. The fall damaged identity but did not erase it. Scripture is, in many ways, God's long story of restoring people to the truth of who they already were in His heart.

Identity always begins with God's design, not with human interpretation. You are not simply the sum of your experiences or the product of your environment. You are not defined by what was said to you in childhood, nor by the failures you carry, nor by the labels others placed on you. You were formed with intention, crafted with precision, and endowed with dignity before you ever entered this world.

The image of God is not just reflected in the "spiritual" parts of your life. It shows up in your curiosity, your creativity, your compassion, your logic, your humor, your strength, your sensitivity, your ability to love, and your desire for purpose.

Even the parts of you that others misunderstood or minimized may actually be some of the clearest evidence of God's craftsmanship. You are more like Him than you realize.

When identity becomes distorted, so does everything else: purpose, calling, relationships, direction, and even our ability to hear God. But when identity is restored, clarity returns. Confidence returns. Calling becomes visible. Purpose becomes attainable. Peace becomes possible. Identity is the soil in which every other part of your life grows.

This is why Genesis begins not with human achievement but with divine intention. God wants you to know that you were made on purpose and with purpose. Your life is not random. Your personality is not accidental. Your desires are not meaningless. Your gifts are not incidental. Every part of you carries the fingerprints of your Creator.

This book is a journey back to that first truth. Through Scripture, story, and reflection, we will walk step-by-step through what I call the Design Discovery Journey—a pathway that helps you recognize how God formed you, what He placed within you, how He motivates you, how He expresses Himself through you, and how your life reflects His grace in the world. You will meet biblical characters—some familiar, some overlooked—whose lives reveal how God forms people intentionally and differently.

At the end of each chapter, you will write a single sentence, a simple reflection that captures one piece of your identity. These pieces will come together in the final chapter as your own Design Discovery Declaration—a personal, powerful summary of who God created you to be.

So today, we begin where Scripture begins: with identity. Before we talk about calling, gifts, desires, or purpose, we anchor ourselves in this foundational truth: you are made in the image of God. And because God does not make junk, there is nothing insignificant, defective, or forgotten about your design.

Take a moment here. Breathe deeply. Let this truth settle into places where lies have lived for too long. You are an image-bearer of the living God.

Reflection for Chapter 1: In the Image of God

Scriptures to Review: Genesis 1:26–31, Psalm 139:13–16, Psalm 8:3–5, Ephesians 4:24

• When you hear 'made in God's image,' what emotions rise in you?

____

____

• Where have you struggled to believe you are 'good'?

____

____

• What parts of your personality feel most God-given?

____

____

Design Discovery Reflection (Puzzle Piece #1):

Because I bear God's image, I reflect Him most clearly when I:

____

____

Chapter 2

Good Saw It Was Good: Living from Blessing, Not Brokenness

Before humanity ever took a step, made a choice, or breathed a prayer, God spoke a word over them that still echoes across history: good. Not "barely acceptable." Not "almost there." Not "promising if you work harder." Good. This was the posture of God toward His creation from the very beginning. His first vision of humanity was one of delight, affirmation, and blessing.

"God saw all that He had made, and it was very good." — Genesis 1:31

It's difficult for many people to believe this about themselves. We are far more accustomed to hearing the opposite—externally or internally. Somewhere along the way, the purity of God's original blessing became buried under a mountain of messages telling us we are not enough. Not thin enough. Not smart enough. Not spiritual enough. Not strong enough. Not gifted enough. Not lovable enough. And without realizing it, we begin to operate from a place of deep insecurity, as if God's first word over humanity had been a criticism rather than a blessing.

But blessing—not brokenness—was the atmosphere in which humanity was meant to live.

Even after the fall, when sin had scarred creation, God did not abandon His posture of blessing. Noah's story is a reminder of this. At a moment when the world was full of corruption, God still chose a man to carry forward His redemptive plan. This wasn't because Noah was perfect; Scripture never says that. Noah found favor because of God's heart, not his own perfection. Even after devastation, God reaffirmed His commitment: creation was still worth restoring, humanity was still worth saving, and the image of God was still worth redeeming.

The blessing was never revoked.

But many of us grew up believing the opposite. We were shaped by voices—sometimes loud, sometimes subtle—that told us we were flawed, unlovable, disappointing, or insufficient. Some of these voices came from family. Others came from culture. Some came from the church. Still others came from our own internal dialogue. Over time, these messages calcify into identity statements:

"I'm broken."

"I'm a failure."

"I'll never be enough."

"Something is wrong with me."

"God must be disappointed in me."

But when God looked at humanity, His first response was joy. His first words were blessing. His first posture was delight.

To reclaim your identity, you must reclaim God's original tone toward you.

God did not begin His relationship with humanity with a list of requirements. He began with approval. He began with goodness. He began with blessing. And if we do not return to this foundational truth, every attempt to understand our gifts, desires, calling, and design will be clouded by shame. Shame distorts everything. It keeps us from seeing our value, recognizing our wiring, or believing anything good about ourselves. Shame whispers, "It can't be good." God whispers, "It already is."

When we look at ourselves through the lens of shame, we see only the parts that feel inadequate or unfinished. But when God looks at us, He sees His image, His delight, His intentional design—and yes, His ongoing work of redemption. God is neither surprised nor discouraged by the places in us that are still becoming. He always begins with blessing, even as He continues to bring us into wholeness.

You were created in blessing.

You were named in blessing.

You were intended for blessing.

And no amount of brokenness can erase the original design of God's goodness in you.

The tragedy is that most people live from their wounds rather than from their blessing. They carry childhood messages into adulthood and interpret their identity through the filter of pain rather than the truth of Genesis 1. But Scripture invites you to return to the beginning—not the beginning of your life, but the beginning of all life. To hear again the very first words God ever spoke over humanity. To let those words wash over the labeling, comparison, judgment, and insecurity that have attached themselves to your story.

You cannot understand your design until you understand your goodness.

This is not the cheap, surface-level affirmation the world offers. It is not a humanistic "believe in yourself" sentiment. It is the theological truth that the God of the universe looked at what He made in you and said, "This is good." He did not say you are flawless. He did not say you will never struggle. He did not say you would not need redemption. But He did say you were worth creating, worth loving, and worth redeeming.

God's blessing is not a reward for good behavior. It is the soil in which identity grows.

When you begin from blessing, everything changes. You stop trying to earn God's approval because you realize you already have it. You stop trying to prove your worth because you recognize it was given to you before time began. You stop disqualifying yourself because you see that God has never disqualified you. And you stop believing the lie that you are too broken to be used by God because He has always chosen imperfect people to fulfill His perfect purposes.

If Genesis 1 teaches us anything about identity, it is that God does not begin with what is wrong. He begins with what is right. And He invites you to do the same.

Take a moment to breathe this in—not academically, not theologically, but personally. God calls you good. God sees the parts of you that you dismiss or criticize, and He calls them good. God sees the strengths you overlook, the qualities you minimize, the beauty you fail to notice—and He calls them good. Let this truth begin softening the places where shame has been hardened for too long.

You were created in goodness.

You were blessed before you were broken.

And God's blessing still rests upon you today.

Reflection for Chapter 2: Called Good

Scriptures to Review: Genesis 1:31, Psalm 139:17–18, Romans 8:1, James 1:18

- What words have shaped how you see yourself?

____

____

- What would it feel like to believe God calls you good?

____

____

- Where have you agreed with a lie instead of truth?

____

____

Design Discovery Reflection (Puzzle Piece #2):

God calls me good, and the goodness I most often overlook in myself:

____

____

Chapter 3
Fearfully and Wonderfully Made

One of the most stunning truths in Scripture is that God did not simply create humanity in general—He created you specifically. Not as a mass-produced life, not as a generic personality, not as a random collection of traits, but as an intentional, handcrafted work of divine artistry. You were formed by a God who does nothing accidentally, nothing carelessly, nothing without purpose.

Psalm 139 pulls back the curtain on this intimate work of God. Here David speaks not as a king, not as a warrior, not as a poet—but as a human being overwhelmed by the realization that God was involved in every detail of his formation. "For You created my inmost being; You knit me together in my mother's womb." God did not simply speak you into existence; He formed you, stitch by stitch, layer by layer, with attention, with affection, with intention.

There is a tenderness in the language David chooses. "Knit me together" suggests careful movement, deliberate craftsmanship, and a pace slow enough to express love. God did not rush your formation. He did not assemble you from spare parts. He wove you. He shaped your personality, your mind, your temperament, your instincts, your strengths, and even your sensitivities with the steady hands of a Master Creator.

And David's response to this realization is simple and profound: "I praise You because I am fearfully and wonderfully made." He didn't say he was perfect. He didn't say he was flawless. He didn't say he was always confident. He simply acknowledged that God's work in forming him was awe-inspiring. Fearfully made. Wonderfully made. Words spoken not out of vanity, but out of revelation.

But for many people today, these words feel almost impossible to believe. We are far more comfortable calling ourselves flawed, inadequate, or disappointing than wonderful. We are quicker to point out what we lack than what God has crafted within us. Somewhere along the way, we learned to distrust our design. We learned to apologize for it. We learned to hide it. We learned to silence it.

But David invites us into a different posture—the posture of seeing ourselves through God's eyes rather than through the distorted lens of insecurity, comparison, or past pain.

David's life itself is a testimony of how God forms people in hidden, intimate places long before anyone else notices. Before he ever faced Goliath, before he ever held a crown, before anyone recognized his potential, David had already been designed and prepared by God. A shepherd boy in the fields, unseen by society, unnoticed by family, was being shaped for a purpose no one else could see.

This is why David could write so confidently about God's involvement in his inner life—he had lived it. His experiences in obscurity were not wasted. His personality, his imagination, his musicality, his courage, his sensitivity, and his leadership instincts were all formed long before they were recognized. God had been shaping his heart when no one else was paying attention.

The same is true for you.

You were made in the quiet places of God's creativity. You were formed in the hidden workshop of His intention. Your wiring is not random. Your personality is not a mistake. Your emotions are not a nuisance. Your instincts are not irrelevant. Your uniqueness is not a liability. Everything about you—yes, everything—was crafted with purpose.

You were fearfully made, which means your design carries the weight of reverence.

You were wonderfully made, which means your design carries the beauty of uniqueness.

But for many of us, the disconnect comes from not knowing what parts of us reflect God's design and what parts reflect wounds or fear. We confuse insecurity with humility. We confuse shame with self-awareness. We confuse trauma with identity. And sometimes, we even confuse the opinions of others with the voice of God.

But here is the truth Psalm 139 calls you back to:

God has never been confused about who He made you to be.

He knows your frame.

He knows your inner wiring.

He knows your personality and your pace.

He knows your passions and your sensitivities.

He knows your strengths and the places where you still need healing.

And He calls all of it "wonderful."

The journey of discovering who God made you to be is not a journey of becoming someone different—it is a journey of becoming someone true. Someone original. Someone formed by the loving hands of God Himself.

You do not need to imitate someone else.

You do not need to apologize for your differences.

You do not need to hide your depth, your softness, your intensity, or your creativity.

You do not need to trade in your God-designed personality for a more "acceptable" one.

God did not knit you together to become a copy.

He formed you to reflect a facet of Himself that no one else reflects quite the same.

If you pay attention, you will begin to see evidence of His craftsmanship everywhere in your life—not just in your talents, but in the subtle details of how you think, how you feel, how you respond, how you imagine, how you love, how you serve, how you see the world.

Identity becomes clearer not by striving, but by recognizing.

Not by changing who you are, but by discovering who you already are.

Let yourself linger in the wonder of this truth. God formed you. God intended you. God took His time with you. You are the result of divine artistry. And that alone is enough to change how you see your life, your worth, and your purpose.

Reflection for Chapter 3: Formed with Intention

Scriptures to Review: Psalm 139:13–16, Jeremiah 1:5, Isaiah 64:8, Ephesians 2:10

- What details about your life feel intentional?

____

____

- What do you consistently gravitate toward?

____

____

- What makes you feel most yourself?

____

____

Design Discovery Reflection (Puzzle Piece #3):

One part of my design that shows God's intentional craftsmanship is:

____

____

Chapter 4
Known Before Birth

There's something comforting—almost unbelievable—about the thought that God knew you before anyone else did. Before you had a name, before your personality took shape, before anyone imagined who you might become, God already knew you. Not in a distant, general sense, but in a personal, intimate way.

Most of us don't think of ourselves like that. We tend to believe our identity started when we were born, when our families first held us, or when the world first began noticing us. But according to Scripture, your story started long before that moment.

When God spoke to Jeremiah, He wasn't just talking to a prophet. He was revealing something true about every human being He creates: "Before I formed you in the womb, I knew you."

Sit with that for a moment.

God knew you.

Before your personality.

Before your choices.

Before your mistakes.

Before your fears.

Before your strengths.

You were known before you were formed.

Jeremiah didn't know what to do with that. His first reaction was to point out everything he wasn't. "I don't know how to speak. I'm too young." He looked at his inadequacies and assumed God must have overlooked them. But God wasn't surprised. He wasn't second-guessing. He wasn't picking someone and hoping for the best.

God knew exactly who Jeremiah was—and exactly who he would become.

Maybe you've had similar thoughts.

"Surely God couldn't use someone like me."

"Maybe who I am isn't enough."

“If God really knew me, He’d choose someone better.”

But that’s just it. God does know you—and He still chose you. He still formed you. He still set you apart with purpose woven into the very beginning of your being.

And here’s the part that might surprise you: the things about yourself that you’ve carried since childhood—the sensitivities, the longings, the instincts, the things that make your heart light up or break—those aren’t random. They didn’t come from nowhere. They’ve been with you because they started with God.

Maybe you’ve always felt deeply.

Maybe you’ve always been drawn to beauty or justice or leadership or creativity.

Maybe you’ve always noticed the people on the edges.

Maybe you’ve always asked deeper questions than your peers.

Maybe you've always carried a quiet burden for someone or something.

Those are early signs of your design.

But life has a way of making us doubt those early hints. Sometimes we're told we're "too much" or "too sensitive" or "too intense" or "too emotional" or "too curious." Sometimes we learn to silence parts of ourselves because they weren't affirmed. Sometimes we bury those original threads so deep that we forget they were ever there.

But God hasn't forgotten.

The truth is, discovering your calling and identity is often less about becoming someone new and more about remembering who you were in the beginning—before fear shaped you, before comparison muted you, before pressure reshaped you.

That's what God was reminding Jeremiah:

"You are not becoming someone I didn't already see. You are stepping into who you've always been."

If you pause long enough and look back, you may recognize patterns—little echoes of who you are today showing up in who you've always been. Maybe you were the child who comforted others. Or the one who asked endless questions. Or the one who organized everything. Or the one who dreamed big. Or the one who wrote stories. Or the one who noticed details no one else saw.

Those weren't just personality quirks. They were clues.

Clues that you were known.

Clues that you were formed.

Clues that God planted something in you before you ever took your first breath.

The truth is: you didn't stumble into who you are. You were shaped that way. And the same God who formed you then is the One who is calling you now.

Reflection for Chapter 4: God-Given Desires
Scriptures to Review: Psalm 37:4, Philippians 2:13, Proverbs 16:3, John 15:7–8

• What longings have stayed with you through the years?

___

___

• Which desires feel 'too big,' yet never leave?

___

___

• What activities awaken something alive in you?

___

___

Design Discovery Reflection (Puzzle Piece #4):

A desire or sensitivity God has placed in me since early life is:

___

___

Chapter 5

Called Through Weakness

Most of us are pretty aware of our weaknesses. In fact, we're usually more aware of what we can't do than what we can. We can list our flaws without hesitation. We know our insecurities by heart. And often, when we even begin to sense that God might want to use us in some way, those weaknesses rush to the front of our mind like an army shouting, "Not you. Not with this. Not with who you are."

If that sounds familiar, you're in good company. Moses felt the exact same way.

When God called Moses from the burning bush, Moses didn't respond with excitement or confidence. He panicked. He argued. He explained all the reasons God had chosen the wrong person. He pointed to his limitations, his inadequacies, his past failures, and the areas where he felt least capable.

"I'm not a good speaker."

"What if they don't believe me?"

"I'm not the right person."

It's almost humorous how determined Moses was to convince God that He'd made a mistake. But God didn't back off. He didn't apologize for calling him. He didn't say, "You know what? You're right. Let me find someone more qualified." Instead, God met every insecurity Moses had—not by removing the weakness, but by promising His presence.

Because here's something important:

God doesn't call you because of your strengths. He calls you because of His purpose.

We tend to assume that God works best through the impressive parts of our lives. Our talents. Our achievements. Our confidence. Our polished areas. But Scripture tells a different story. Time and time again, God chooses to work through the places that feel most fragile.

Why?

Because weakness has a way of keeping us dependent. It keeps us humble. It keeps us aware that whatever God does in us or through us isn't because of our perfection—it's because of His grace.

Weakness becomes the soil where God's strength can actually take root.

Moses' perceived weakness—his insecurity about speaking—became the very place God showed His power. And interestingly, the thing Moses thought disqualified him didn't stop his calling at all. In fact, Moses' voice—trembling or not—became the voice that confronted kings, comforted a nation, and carried God's message.

So maybe the things you see as weaknesses aren't actually barriers to God's plan. Maybe they're invitations.

Maybe the insecurity you're ashamed of is the very thing God wants to redeem.

Maybe the fear you carry is not a disqualifier, but a doorway.

Maybe the limitation you obsess over is the place where God plans to show His strength.

None of this means God celebrates our pain or excuses our wounds. It means He wastes nothing. He can use the places that seem least usable because nothing about your design surprises Him—not the strong parts and not the weak ones.

Think about your life for a moment. What have you tried to hide? What do you wish wasn't part of your story? What do you try to overcome before you feel "ready" for God to use you?

Sometimes the places we try the hardest to cover are the ones God wants to uncover. Not to expose us, but to empower us. Weakness often becomes the doorway to calling because it forces us to rely on God in ways strength never will.

And let's be honest—sometimes our greatest gifts grow in the shadow of our greatest insecurities. A compassionate heart often forms through seasons of feeling overlooked. A strong voice often rises from years of silence. A leader is often shaped through seasons of uncertainty. The weakness doesn't cancel the calling; it shapes it.

God didn't choose Moses in spite of his weakness.

He chose Moses with full awareness of it.

And He chooses you the same way.

You don't need to have all your insecurities solved before God can use you. You don't need to have full confidence before taking a step. You don't need to be the strongest voice in the room, the most talented person in your circle, or the most impressive option on the table.

God never asked Moses to be impressive.

He only asked him to be willing.

And God is asking the same from you.

Reflection for Chapter 5: Strengths by Design

Scriptures to Review: Romans 12:6–8, 1 Peter 4:10, 1 Corinthians 12:4–7, Exodus 35:30–35

• What comes naturally to you?

• What do others affirm in you?

• When do you feel most effective or energized?

Design Discovery Reflection (Puzzle Piece #5):

A weakness or insecurity God may actually want to use in my calling is:

Chapter 6
Positioned for Purpose

There are moments in life when you look around and wonder, "How did I end up here?" Sometimes that question comes from a place of gratitude, and other times from confusion or even frustration. But underneath the question is something deeper: a longing to know whether where you are actually matters.

We don't always think of our location—our job, our community, our season of life—as part of God's design. Most of us assume purpose comes from dramatic callings or obvious gifts. But Scripture shows us something different: God often works through ordinary placement long before we recognize the meaning in it.

No story captures this better than Esther's.

When Esther became queen, she wasn't trying to fulfill a calling. She wasn't campaigning for influence. She wasn't seeking a platform. She wasn't even from the social class that typically shaped history. She was simply living the life in front of her—navigating circumstances she never asked for and stepping into places she didn't choose.

And yet, she was exactly where she needed to be.

When the threat against her people surfaced, Esther didn't feel courageous or qualified. In fact, her instinct was fear. She didn't see herself as someone God could use. She didn't even know if she had the right to speak up. But her cousin Mordecai saw what she couldn't see:

"Who knows but that you have come to your royal position for such a time as this?"

In other words:

"Esther, what if you're not here by accident?"

That question changed everything.

And maybe it changes something for you too.

We often overlook the possibility that God has positioned us where we are—right now, in this season, with these people, in this environment—for reasons we don't yet understand. We imagine calling requires a big stage or bold confidence, but

God frequently works through subtle placement long before He works through visible gifts.

Sometimes God puts you somewhere not because you feel ready, but because the moment needs the version of you that already exists.

Your job.

Your friendships.

Your neighborhood.

Your family.

Your community.

Your season—whether it feels exciting, mundane, or uncomfortable.

Any of these may be part of a larger story God is writing.

But here's the thing: when we don't feel particularly strong or spiritual or qualified, it becomes easy to believe our placement doesn't matter. Esther felt that too. She didn't feel powerful. She didn't feel prepared. She didn't feel influential. But she was positioned. And God used her placement before He ever used her confidence.

Maybe the same is true for you.

Maybe the reason you're in a certain workplace is because someone there needs your compassion or courage.

Maybe the reason you're in this city—or this small town—is because God is building something in you that couldn't grow anywhere else.

Maybe the reason you've walked through particular experiences is because someone else will need the wisdom you gained.

Maybe the reason you're surrounded by certain people is because you're carrying a light they don't have yet.

Calling rarely begins with clarity. It often begins with location.

And sometimes we don't recognize the divine threading until much later. When you look back on your life, you may see moments where your placement didn't feel spiritual—it just felt… real.

Maybe even painful or confusing. And yet those places shaped you. Positioned you. Prepared you.

Esther's story reminds us that God is always working behind the scenes, arranging details we don't see, placing people in the right moments, and weaving stories that will eventually reveal His purpose.

So instead of asking, "Why am I here?"

Try asking, "What if God has me here for a reason?"

The shift may be small, but the impact is huge.

The moment you begin to see your placement as intentional—even when it's imperfect—your perspective changes. You stop waiting for some future moment of purpose and start recognizing the possibility in your present one. You start noticing the people around you differently. You start paying attention to conversations, opportunities, burdens, and nudges in your heart.

You start to wonder, "What if this is my moment? What if this is my place?"

Esther needed courage to step into her purpose, but she didn't need clarity before she acted. She just needed to trust that her placement was part of God's design.

Your placement matters too. Even if you don't fully understand why you're here—or why you're here now—you can trust that God is not careless with your life. He positions His people with purpose.

Reflection for Chapter 6: God at Work in Weakness

Scriptures to Review: 2 Corinthians 12:9–10, Romans 8:26, Isaiah 40:29–31, Corinthians 1:27–29

- What areas of your life feel tender or fragile?

____

____

- Where has God met you most deeply in weakness?

____

____

- How has struggle shaped your compassion?

____

____

Design Discovery Reflection (Puzzle Piece #6):

A circumstance or placement in my life that may be strategic is:

____

____

Chapter 7
Shaped in Hidden Places

There are seasons in life when it feels like nothing is happening. You're doing the right things—showing up, being faithful, putting in effort—but it seems like no one notices. No doors open. No spotlight shines. No affirmation arrives. It's just you, your ordinary responsibilities, and a quiet sense that you were made for something… but you're not sure what.

Those seasons can be frustrating. Sometimes even painful. But hidden seasons are not wasted seasons. In fact, they are often the most important chapters of your story.

Ask David.

When we think of David, we imagine the king—the warrior, the poet, the man after God's own heart. But David didn't start with a throne. He didn't start with followers. He didn't even start with recognition from his own family. David's story began in the fields, taking care of sheep while everyone else lived more public lives.

When Samuel came to anoint the next king of Israel, David wasn't even invited to the gathering. Think about that. The most important conversation in the nation's future was happening in his own home, and he wasn't considered valuable enough to be included.

But God saw him.

And God had been shaping him long before anyone else cared to look.

David's hidden life—those years of quiet faithfulness—were not a detour. They were preparation. He learned to fight lions and bears long before he ever stood in front of Goliath. He learned to worship in solitude long before he led a nation in worship. He learned courage, humility, patience, and trust in the secret place long before he carried responsibility in the public one.

David's most significant strengths were formed in obscurity, not visibility.

And the same is true for you.

Most of the time, we assume that progress is visible. We assume growth means movement, promotion, recognition, or new opportunities. But some of God's best work happens underground, where roots grow deep even when nothing seems to be happening on the surface.

Hidden seasons teach us to depend on God instead of applause.

They teach us to grow character instead of image.

They teach us to listen for God's voice instead of chasing validation.

They teach us to serve without being seen—and to trust that God sees even when others don't.

And here's the beautiful thing: hidden seasons often reveal gifts we would never have discovered otherwise. In the quiet, we learn what stirs our heart. In the silence, we hear what truly matters. In the stillness, we find out who we are when no one is watching.

Maybe you're in a hidden season right now. Maybe you feel unseen, unnoticed, or overlooked. Maybe you've wondered if your life is moving at all. But hidden doesn't mean forgotten. Hidden doesn't mean unimportant. Hidden doesn't mean God has paused your purpose.

Hidden means God is shaping you privately so you can carry what He gives you publicly.

David wasn't waiting for his "real life" to begin. He was becoming the person who could handle the future God was preparing for him. He learned courage in the fields. He learned integrity in the fields. He learned worship in the fields. The fields were not a lesser place—they were a shaping place.

What if your current season—no matter how quiet or uneventful it feels—is doing the same for you?

What if the things you're learning now will become the backbone of your calling later?

What if the qualities being formed in you today are the very ones God will use tomorrow?

What if this "ordinary" season is actually forming extraordinary strength?

Sometimes the most powerful parts of our design are shaped when no one is watching.

God does some of His deepest work in hidden places because He knows hidden does not mean insignificant—it means intimate. It means He has you close enough to shape without distraction.

And just like David, your hidden seasons are preparing you for moments you haven't seen yet. Moments where courage will be required. Moments where faith will need to rise. Moments where character will matter more than talent. Moments where your heart—the one God formed in the quiet—will define how you lead, love, serve, and show up in the world.

Reflection for Chapter 7: Shaped in Hidden Places

Scriptures to Review: 1 Samuel 16:1–13, Psalm 32:7, Matthew 6:6, 1 Peter 5:6

- What hidden seasons have shaped you?

____

____

- What did God develop in you during quiet years?

____

____

- How has obscurity strengthened your soul?

____

____

Design Discovery Reflection (Puzzle Piece #7):

From my hidden seasons, God developed in me:

____

____

Chapter 8
Shaped Through Adversity

If we're honest, adversity rarely feels meaningful while we're living through it. Most of the time, it just feels hard. Painful. Unfair. Confusing. We wonder if we've done something wrong, or if God has forgotten us, or if we somehow missed the turn that would have led to an easier life. When we're in the middle of struggle, it's difficult to imagine that anything good could come from it.

But adversity has a strange way of revealing what comfort never will.

Sometimes the hardest seasons of our lives become the ones that shape us most deeply. Not because the pain was good, but because God is so good that He refuses to waste the pain.

Joseph's story is proof of that.

When Joseph was a teenager, he had dreams—big ones. He believed God had a purpose for his life, and he wasn't wrong. But what Joseph didn't know was the path that purpose would take. Before the dream ever came true, Joseph was betrayed by his brothers, thrown into a pit, sold as a slave, falsely accused, imprisoned, forgotten, overlooked, and repeatedly disappointed.

It would have been easy for him to believe the dream was dead.

Or worse—that something was wrong with him.

That God had changed His mind.

That adversity meant abandonment.

But it didn't.

God was shaping Joseph the entire time.

Every betrayal taught him wisdom.

Every disappointment deepened his compassion.

Every setback strengthened his resilience.

Every lonely season prepared his character for the weight of the future.

Every injustice refined his leadership.

Every adversity formed something in him that prosperity never could.

By the time Joseph stood in front of Pharaoh, ready to interpret a dream that would save nations, he wasn't just talented—he was prepared. He had become the kind of man who could handle influence without losing humility, power without losing perspective, authority without losing compassion.

Adversity shaped him into someone who could carry the dream responsibly.

Your adversity may be doing the same for you.

This doesn't mean God causes every painful thing in your life. But it does mean He can use every painful thing in your life. He can take what was meant to destroy you and use it to develop you. He can take seasons of heartbreak, loss, rejection, confusion, or difficulty and work them into the soil of your identity, forming strength, empathy, courage, and clarity that would never have formed otherwise.

Some of the most powerful parts of your design—the compassion you carry, the wisdom you've gained, the strength you've built, the resilience that's grown in you—were shaped in adversity.

Think about the hardest moments you've lived through.

The seasons where you felt stretched thin.

The relationships that broke your heart.

The disappointments that shook your confidence.

The failures that humbled you.

The transitions that unsettled you.

If you look closely, you may notice something surprising: you are not the same person you were before those seasons. Something in you grew. Something in you deepened. Something in you strengthened.

Adversity has a way of forming us from the inside out.

Joseph eventually stood in front of the very brothers who betrayed him. Only now, he wasn't a wounded teenager desperate for validation—he was a mature man who understood the purpose behind his pain. He said, "You intended to harm me, but God intended it for good."

That's not the voice of someone who avoided adversity.

That's the voice of someone transformed by it.

When Joseph forgave his brothers, he wasn't excusing their actions. He was recognizing that God had done something in him that was bigger than the hurt he had endured.

Maybe God is doing something similar in you.

Maybe the season you thought would break you is the season that's been building you.

Maybe what you survived is preparing you for the person you're becoming.

Maybe the very thing you wish had never happened is shaping the part of you God plans to use most.

Adversity doesn't define you, but it does refine you.

When you allow God to meet you in your pain, the hardship becomes holy ground. Not because the suffering was holy, but because God stepped into it with you—and shaped something profound within you through it.

Reflection for Chapter 8: Shaped Through Adversity

Scriptures to Review: Genesis 50:20, James 1:2–4, Romans 5:3–5, 2 Corinthians 4:8–10

• What adversity marked your life?

____

____

• What unexpected strength came from it?

____

____

• What do you now understand that you didn't then?

____

____

Design Discovery Reflection (Puzzle Piece #8):

A hardship that shaped me for greater purpose is:

____

____

Chapter 9
You Are God's Workmanship

There are days when it's easy to believe God is doing something beautiful in your life. Days when things click, when you feel purposeful, when your heart is full, when circumstances line up in a way that makes sense. On those days, "God's workmanship" feels true.

But then there are the other days—the messy ones. The uncertain ones. The "I thought I'd be further along by now" ones. The days when you wonder if you're growing at all. When you feel stuck, unseen, discouraged, or confused. On those days, it's hard to imagine your life looks anything like a masterpiece.

Yet Scripture doesn't say you feel like God's workmanship.

It says you are.

"We are God's workmanship, created in Christ Jesus to do good works, which God prepared in advance for us to do." — Ephesians 2:10

That word "workmanship" comes from the Greek poiēma, where we get our word "poem." It means something intentionally crafted, something skillfully shaped, something with thought behind every detail.

That means you are not a product of randomness.

You are not a collection of traits that happened to land in one person.

You are not a cosmic accident with a spiritual destiny attached later.

You are God's artwork—designed with vision, crafted with care, shaped with intention.

Paul understood this better than most, because his own story was a masterpiece in progress. Before he became the apostle who wrote much of the New Testament, Paul was Saul—a man convinced he was serving God while actually wounding God's people. His life was moving in completely the wrong direction. His identity was wrapped in performance and zeal, but his heart was hardened. If anyone seemed far from purpose, it was Saul.

But that didn't stop God.

When God confronted Saul on the road to Damascus, He didn't discard him—He redirected him. He didn't shame him—He transformed him. God took the fiery passion that had once harmed others and redirected that same passion toward healing, teaching, and building the church. The very intensity that made Saul dangerous became the exact intensity that made Paul effective.

God didn't erase Saul's personality.

He redeemed it.

That's what it means to be God's workmanship. God doesn't start from scratch—He starts from you. Who you already are. Who He already formed. Who He already sees. Even the parts you think are liabilities can become strengths when shaped by God's hands.

And here's the part many people miss:

God's workmanship happens over time.

You're not a finished painting yet.

You're a work in progress—layer by layer, color by color, stroke by stroke.

Some seasons add brightness.

Some add depth.

Some add shadow or texture.

Some add contrast.

But all of them add meaning.

When you look at your life, you might be tempted to judge it by a single season—a struggle, a mistake, a battle, a disappointment. But a single brushstroke doesn't define a painting. When God sees your life, He sees the full canvas. He sees what He's shaping, not just what's unfinished.

And He calls the process beautiful.

Think about the parts of your story that feel rough or unfinished. Maybe there are moments you wish you could erase. Maybe there are chapters you wish never happened. Maybe there are habits or patterns you're still asking God to heal. Even those places can become part of the artwork when surrendered to Him.

Paul's greatest source of shame became part of his testimony.

His past didn't disqualify him—it illuminated God's grace.

The same might be true for you.

You are not beyond God's ability to shape you.

You are not behind schedule.

You are not too messy to be meaningful.

You are not too unfinished to be useful.

You are being crafted.

And here's something important: as God shapes you, He prepares specific good works for you—things only you can do, in ways only you can do them, because of the exact way He designed you.

Your story matters.

Your wiring matters.

Your experiences matter.

Your personality matters.

Your strengths and your struggles both matter.

Reflection for Chapter 9: God's Workmanship

Scriptures to Review: Ephesians 2:10, Philippians 1:6, Romans 12:2, 2 Corinthians 3:18

• Which parts of your story carry God's fingerprints?

____

____

• Where have you seen transformation?

____

____

• What chapter once felt painful but now feels purposeful?

____

____

Design Discovery Reflection (Puzzle Piece #9):

A part of my story that reveals God's craftsmanship is:

____

____

Chapter 10
One Body, Many Members

If you've ever compared yourself to someone else and felt smaller, less valuable, or somehow "not enough," you're not alone. We live in a world where comparison is almost effortless. It creeps in through our friendships, our families, our workplaces, and especially our churches. Somewhere deep down, we begin to believe the lie that our worth is connected to how we measure up to someone else.

But Scripture paints a completely different picture of how God sees us—and how He designed community to function.

Paul writes in 1 Corinthians 12 that the Body of Christ is made up of many members, each with a different gift, different role, and different function. And every part is essential.

The eye can't say to the hand, "I don't need you."

The head can't say to the feet, "You don't matter."

And yet, many of us say those very things to ourselves.

We tell ourselves someone else is more spiritual, more gifted, more impactful, more useful. We downplay what God has placed inside us because it doesn't look like what He placed inside someone else. But God didn't create a world filled with duplicates. He created a body—a living, breathing spiritual ecosystem—where every member contributes something that would be missing without them.

Imagine trying to walk without your ankle. Or trying to see without your eyelids. Or trying to breathe without your diaphragm. None of these parts get much attention, but without them, everything collapses.

In the same way, there is something about you—some way God works through you—that others may never notice at first glance, but the Kingdom would feel the loss if you weren't offering it.

Barnabas is a perfect example of this.

Barnabas wasn't the loudest apostle. He didn't write letters like Paul. He didn't preach with the fire of Peter. He didn't have the dramatic conversion story. In fact, he rarely stood in the spotlight. But Barnabas had a gift that shaped the early church in a profound way: encouragement.

When everyone else was afraid of Paul, Barnabas stood beside him. When John Mark failed and disappointed Paul, Barnabas defended him, restored him, and eventually helped him become useful again. Without Barnabas, half the New Testament might never have been written—because Paul may never have been encouraged into leadership, and John Mark may never have recovered from failure.

Barnabas reminds us that "less visible" does not mean "less valuable."

Your gift doesn't have to be dramatic to be essential.

Your contribution doesn't have to be loud to be powerful.

Your impact doesn't have to be public to be meaningful.

Sometimes the gifts that operate behind the scenes create the greatest ripple effects.

Maybe your gift is hospitality—making people feel seen and welcomed.

Maybe it's wisdom—helping others make sense of their questions.

Maybe it's mercy—sitting with people in their pain.

Maybe it's leadership—bringing clarity and direction when others feel lost.

Maybe it's administration—bringing calm to chaos so ministry can flourish.

Maybe it's encouragement—lifting weary hearts at the exact moment they want to give up.

Maybe it's generosity—seeing needs before others do.

Maybe it's intercession—carrying people in prayer when they can't carry themselves.

Whatever your gift is, it matters.

And here's something freeing:

You don't have to possess every gift. You only have to steward the one God gave you.

Paul goes on to say that God Himself arranges the members of the body exactly as He wills. That means your gift isn't random. Your wiring isn't random. Your contribution isn't random. God placed you where He wanted you with the gift He wanted you to have.

And this is where identity becomes so important.

You can't walk confidently in your gift if you're busy wishing you had someone else's.

Comparison kills calling. Jealousy kills joy.

Insecurity kills contribution.

But clarity—clarity sets you free.

When you recognize how God naturally expresses Himself through you, you stop competing and start contributing. You stop comparing and start offering. You stop minimizing and start realizing that God designed you to bring something to the body that no one else brings in quite the same way.

Different doesn't mean lesser. Different means needed.

Every gift matters because every person matters.

And you—yes, you—are part of a divine design bigger than anything you can see right now.

Reflection for Chapter 10: One Body, Many Members

Scriptures to Review: 1 Corinthians 12:12–27, Romans 12:4–6, Ephesians 4:15–16, 1 Peter 4:10–11

• Where do you fit naturally in community?

____

____

• When have you felt 'necessary'?

____

____

• What role feels most like home?

____

____

Design Discovery Reflection (Puzzle Piece #10):

A spiritual gift I see God regularly use in me is:

____

____

Chapter 11

Grace to Speak, Grace to Serve

If you've ever felt like your gift doesn't matter because it doesn't look like someone else's, Peter has a word for you. In his letter, he breaks down spiritual gifts into two simple, powerful categories: speaking gifts and serving gifts. And he doesn't rank them. He doesn't elevate one and diminish the other. He simply says:

"Each of you should use whatever gift you have received to serve others…

If anyone speaks, they should do so as one who speaks the very words of God.

If anyone serves, they should do so with the strength God provides." — 1 Peter 4:10–11

In other words:

Whatever God placed in you—use it. And use it with Him.

Some people feel at home with speaking gifts. They communicate clearly. They encourage boldly. They teach, inspire, explain, comfort, or bring clarity through words. Their voice becomes a vessel for God's heart.

Others feel more at home with serving gifts. They notice needs no one else sees. They help without hesitation. They bring order, kindness, support, or strength in ways that often go unnoticed but always go unmatched. Their actions become a channel of God's love.

Both are sacred.

Both are powerful.

Both are needed.

But sometimes, we undervalue one or the other—usually the one we hold.

People with speaking gifts sometimes feel pressure to always have the right words.

People with serving gifts sometimes feel invisible or secondary.

People with administrative gifts think they're "not spiritual enough."

People with compassion gifts fear they're "too sensitive."

But Peter simplifies everything:

If you speak, speak with God.

If you serve, serve with God.

And in both, God is glorified.

What matters most isn't the category of your gift—it's your connection to the One who gave it.

Take Stephen, for example. He wasn't an apostle. He wasn't a pastor or a prophet. He was chosen to help distribute food to widows. A serving role. A practical role. A role many people would consider "small."

Yet Scripture says Stephen was full of grace and power, performing signs and wonders among the people. Full of wisdom. Full of the Spirit. His serving gift made space for God's presence to move in extraordinary ways, because he didn't treat his role as unimportant. He treated it as sacred.

Imagine what might happen if you began viewing your gift the same way.

Your practical service—the things you think anyone could do—might be the very thing that carries God's presence into someone's life. Your words—spoken over a friend, a coworker, a family member—might become the very words that lift them out of despair. Your encouragement might redirect someone's destiny. Your hospitality might heal someone's loneliness. Your willingness to stay behind the scenes might hold everything together.

Your gift matters deeply—not because it's flashy, but because God is in it.

Peter challenges us not to compare gifts, but to steward them. To recognize that God gives gifts not for our ego, but for the sake of others. Gifts are meant to flow outward.

And here's something important:

You don't have to be amazing at your gift for God to use it.

You just have to offer it.

Peter also reminds us that God provides the strength behind the serving. That means you don't have to rely on your own energy, your own eloquence, or your own ability. When you step into your gift, God steps into you.

Maybe you're someone who feels energized when speaking life over others.

Maybe you come alive when you're quietly helping in ways no one notices.

Maybe your best offering is a prayer whispered in faith.

Maybe your greatest gift is presence—your ability to sit with someone in their pain.

Whatever form your gift takes, God designed it intentionally. You don't need to force it, and you don't need to apologize for it.

Your gift reflects His grace.

Your gift reveals His heart.

Your gift contributes to His Kingdom in ways only you can.

Reflection for Chapter 11: Grace to Speak & Serve

Scriptures to Review: 1 Peter 4:10–11,
Colossians 3:17, 1 Thessalonians 5:11, Galatians 5:13

• Which gift feels more natural — speaking or serving?

____

____

• How does God express His heart through you?

____

____

• Where do you feel His strength most clearly?

____

____

Design Discovery Reflection (Puzzle Piece #11):

A way God expresses Himself through my speaking or serving is:

____

____

Chapter 12

The Greatest of These Is Love

By the time Paul gets to 1 Corinthians 13, he has already spent an entire chapter describing the wide variety of spiritual gifts—and how each one is essential to the Body of Christ. But then he shifts the conversation. It's as if Paul steps back and says, "All of these gifts are beautiful. All of them matter. All of them come from the Spirit. But there is something greater than all of them combined."

Love.

Not love as a feeling.

Not love as politeness.

Not love as sentiment.

Not love as performance.

But love as the very nature of God flowing through His people.

Paul doesn't diminish the value of gifts—he elevates the purpose behind them. Gifts aren't meant to impress; they're meant to express. And what they express, at the deepest level, is the heart of God.

This means something important for your identity:

Your design was never meant to function without love.

You can speak with wisdom, insight, clarity, and power—but without love, Paul says it becomes noise.

You can serve faithfully, generously, tirelessly—but without love, it loses its meaning.

You can sacrifice, give, teach, lead, encourage, or pray—but without love shaping it, the act loses the heart behind it.

Love is not an accessory. It is the operating system of every spiritual gift.

And here's the beautiful part: love looks different through each person's design.

For some, love sounds like encouragement spoken at just the right moment.

For others, love looks like a meal delivered quietly to someone in need.

For some, love feels like leadership that creates safety and direction.

For others, love expresses itself through listening without judgment.

Love is the common thread, but the expression is uniquely you.

Paul goes on to describe what love looks like in real life:

Love is patient.

Love is kind.

Love isn't envious, boastful, arrogant, or rude.

Love isn't easily angered.

Love keeps no record of wrongs.

Love protects, trusts, hopes, and perseveres.

Love never fails.

This isn't just a poetic moment; it's an identity moment.

It's Paul saying: "Everything God designed you to be functions best when rooted in love."

The Corinthians were gifted—but they were also competitive, insecure, self-focused, and easily divided. They wanted their gifts to shine more than they wanted love to flow. And Paul knew that without love, gifting starts to feel like striving, proving, comparing, or performing.

Sound familiar?

Sometimes we chase our gifts so hard that we forget why they exist—to reveal God's heart.

Sometimes we want to be effective more than we want to be loving.

Sometimes our gifts grow faster than our character, and we forget that love is the framework that keeps everything aligned.

But when love becomes the foundation:

Your speaking gifts become healing instead of harsh.

Your serving gifts become joyful instead of exhausting.

Your leadership becomes empowering instead of controlling.

Your compassion becomes wise instead of overwhelming.

Your wisdom becomes gentle instead of intimidating.

Your creativity becomes a blessing instead of a burden.

Love transforms the gift—and the giver.

And here's something freeing:

You don't have to manufacture love. You receive it first.

You can only give what you allow God to form in you.

Your ability to love well grows out of your experience of God's love toward you.

This is why Paul says love never fails—it's anchored in God, not your performance.

As you discover your design—your gifts, your wiring, your passions, your purpose—remember this truth:

The goal is not to become impressive.

The goal is to become loving.

Your identity finds its truest expression not in how gifted you are, but in how well those gifts express God's love through you.

Whatever God designed you to do, however He wired you to serve or speak or lead or listen—it all carries its fullest meaning when rooted in love.

Reflection for Chapter 12: The Greatest of These Is Love

Scriptures to Review: 1 Corinthians 13,
John 13:34–35, 1 John 4:7–12, Romans 12:9–10

• How does love shape your gift?

____

____

• Where is God inviting you into deeper love?

____

____

• What does love look like through your design?

____

____

Design Discovery Reflection (Puzzle Piece #12):

My gift expresses God's love most clearly when I:

____

____

Chapter 13

Your Unique Design

By the time you reach this chapter, something sacred has been unfolding. Little by little, piece by piece, you've been gathering clues about who God created you to be. Not just what you can do, but who you are—your identity, your wiring, your gifts, your burdens, your passions, your patterns, your story.

And somewhere along this journey, a quiet realization may have started forming:

You are uniquely designed.

Not generally.

Not accidentally.

Not vaguely or vaguely defined.

But intentionally—crafted with a combination of traits, experiences, giftings, desires, and hopes that no one else carries in exactly the same way.

Sometimes people imagine discovering their identity as one big "aha" moment. But most of the time, it's more like a slow unfolding. A gentle remembering. A holy noticing.

One puzzle piece at a time.

When you look back at everything we've walked through so far, you may start to see themes emerging:

You bear the image of God.

You were called good from the beginning.

You were formed with intention.

You were known before you were born.

You have desires and sensitivities planted by God Himself.

You carry strengths shaped by design.

You have weaknesses God can work through.

You've been positioned with purpose.

You've been shaped in hidden seasons.

You've been refined through adversity.

You are God's workmanship.

You are essential to the Body of Christ.

You express God's heart through speaking or serving.

You were made to let love lead the way.

These are not random truths—they are threads forming a tapestry.

And that tapestry is you.

One of the most beautiful things about God is that He never mass-produces people. You're not a replica, a rerun, or a recycled version of someone else's assignment. You are an original design—an intentional expression of an infinite God.

And because of that, you don't have to try to be anyone else.

Not their personality.

Not their pace.

Not their calling.

Not their voice.

Not their passion.

Not their expression of faith.

Your design is not meant to imitate—it's meant to illuminate.

Think of all the biblical characters we've explored. None of them looked alike. None of them expressed themselves the same way. None of them fulfilled someone else's calling. They each carried something unique. Something only they could reveal. Something intentionally placed inside them by God:

David revealed God's heart.

Esther revealed God's timing.

Joseph revealed God's sovereignty.

Moses revealed God's patience and power.

Barnabas revealed God's encouragement.

Stephen revealed God's courage.

Paul revealed God's grace.

And now—here's the breathtaking part—you reveal something about God too.

There is a facet of God's heart that shines through you in a way no one else on earth can replicate. Not better or worse—just uniquely yours.

Your compassion may reveal His gentleness.

Your leadership may reveal His steadiness.

Your creativity may reveal His imagination.

Your perseverance may reveal His faithfulness.

Your joy may reveal His delight.

Your generosity may reveal His abundance.

Your discernment may reveal His wisdom.

Your presence may reveal His peace.

Your service may reveal His humility.

This is why your design matters.

This is why your puzzle pieces matter.

This is why the world needs who God created you to be.

Not someday—now.

Not when you're more confident—now.

Not when you've "fixed" yourself—now.

Not when you reach a certain level of spiritual maturity—now.

Your design is already speaking.

Already shining.

Already expressing something divine.

The journey now is learning to recognize it—to see yourself the way God sees you. To embrace your wiring rather than resist it. To honor your design instead of apologizing for it. To offer what God placed inside you instead of comparing it to what He placed inside someone else.

You are not behind.

You are not unqualified.

You are not missing pieces.

Everything God intended for this moment is already within you.

Reflection for Chapter 13: Your Unique Design

Scriptures to Review: Romans 12:4–8,
1 Corinthians 12:4–6, 2 Timothy 1:6, Matthew 5:16

- What theme stands out across your puzzle pieces?

____

____

- What trait feels uniquely you?

____

____

- What part of God's heart do you reflect?

____

____

Design Discovery Reflection (Puzzle Piece #13):

The part of God's heart that I believe my life reveals is:

____

____

Chapter 14
Living from Your Design

You've gathered a lot of pieces on this journey. Not theoretical ideas or abstract theology, but real clues about who you are—how God formed you, how He speaks through you, how He shaped your heart, and how He prepared you through every season of your story. If you've walked slowly through the reflections, you now hold something sacred: a clearer picture of your God-given design. Now comes the question that will shape the rest of your life: What does it look like to live from your design?

Living from your design doesn't mean living a dramatic or world-changing life, though it might. It doesn't mean chasing a specific role or platform, or even suddenly feeling certain about every decision. Living from your design simply means this: you show up as the person God created you to be—on purpose. Not shrinking. Not apologizing. Not comparing. Not striving to become someone else's idea of "enough." Just you—wholehearted, aligned, faithful, and present.

When you begin living this way, you stop fighting your design. You stop calling your strengths "too much" and your sensitivities "not enough." You stop trying to fix parts of yourself God never asked you to fix. You stop resenting the way you're wired. Instead, you honor the way God made you. You let your compassion breathe, your leadership rise, your creativity play, your desire for justice speak, and your gentleness guide. You allow your God-given nature to surface instead of silencing it.

Living from your design also means allowing love to lead. Every gift you carry is meant to express love—God's love moving through you. So you begin asking, "What is the most loving way I can show up as myself today?" Sometimes it's speaking, sometimes it's serving, listening, creating, advocating, or even resting. Love—not pressure, guilt, or performance—becomes the motive.

You also begin to embrace your lane. You stop comparing your calling to someone else's or measuring your worth by someone else's capacity. You stop apologizing for the size, shape, or visibility of your assignment. You understand that your design determines your lane, your lane determines your impact, and your impact is exactly what God intended. Some lanes are wide and loud, others quiet and narrow. All of them are necessary.

As you live from your design, you learn to trust God with the unfolding. You don't have to force outcomes, rush purpose, or make your future happen. Your job is faithfulness; God's job is fruitfulness. Living from your design means releasing the pressure to "be great" and embracing the invitation to be aligned—to live in sync with who God created you to be and trust Him with the story.

Living from your design also means offering your life back to God daily. Your design is not static; it grows, shifts, and matures. Your gifts deepen, your wisdom expands, and your compassion stretches. Your story continues revealing new ways God wants to use you. So you simply keep offering Him your whole self: "God, here I am. Use the way You made me. Let my life reveal Your heart." Simple. Surrendered. Powerful.

And surprisingly, as you begin living from your authentic, God-crafted design, you experience more peace and less anxiety. Much of the pressure, overwhelm, and internal tension we feel doesn't come from life itself. It comes from living out of alignment with who God created us to be—pushing ourselves into roles that don't fit, trying to match someone else's pace, striving to fulfill someone else's calling, or operating outside our gifting out of obligation. When we do that, something inside us strains and feels unsettled, like trying to force a puzzle piece where it doesn't belong. But when you live from your true design, something beautiful happens: your internal resistance loosens, your stress softens, your anxiety quiets, and your soul exhales. You stop fighting yourself. You stop apologizing for how you're wired. You stop carrying the unnecessary burden of becoming someone God never asked you to be. Living from your design won't remove every challenge in life, but it will remove the unnecessary ones—the ones created by working against your God-given rhythm. When you live in alignment with how God made you, life feels less uphill. Decisions feel clearer. Relationships feel more authentic. Days feel more purposeful. This is the peace that comes from working with your design instead of against it—a peace God always intended for you to experience.

When God imagined you, He had a purpose in mind. When He formed you, He placed intentionality in every detail. When He watched you grow, He saw clues to your calling. When He walked with you through adversity, He shaped you. When He saved you, He redeemed your story. When He gifted you, He empowered you. And when He called you, He invited you to live fully as His creation. The world doesn't need a better version of someone else—it needs the full, alive, God-designed version of you.

Living from your design isn't about doing more; it's about being true. Being aligned. Being whole. Being present. Being responsive to God's love. You don't have to wait to begin. Start today. Start small. Start with the next right thing that reflects who God created you to be. You were crafted with intention. You were designed with love. And now, you get to live from that design with freedom.

Reflection for Chapter 14: Living From Your Design

Scriptures to Review: John 10:10, Psalm 37:23–24, Proverbs 3:5–6, Galatians 5:25

• What changes will help you live from your design?

____

____

• Where is God calling you into alignment?

____

____

• What feels lighter now that you understand your wiring?

____

____

Design Discovery Reflection (Puzzle Piece #14):

One way I will intentionally live from my God-given design is:

____

____

Epilogue

Becoming Who You Already Are

By now you've walked through a journey that probably felt less like learning something new and more like remembering something ancient—something true about you that had been waiting beneath the noise, the pressure, the expectations, and the stories you carried.

Piece by piece, chapter by chapter, God has been gently revealing who He designed you to be. Not a future version of you. Not a polished, perfected version of you. But the you He imagined before time, the you He formed with intention, the you He has walked with through every season of your life.

The world around you is loud. It pulls, it pressures, it compares, it demands. It tells you to reinvent yourself, to improve yourself, to hustle your way into worthiness. But none of that creates peace. None of that creates clarity. And none of that brings you closer to the truth.

Because the truth is simple and freeing:

You already are who God created you to be.

Now you are learning to live in agreement with that truth.

You don't have to strive to become beloved—you already are.

You don't have to earn significance—it was spoken over you from the beginning.

You don't have to outrun insecurity—God is re-naming you at a deeper level.

You don't have to "fix" your design—your Creator is teaching you to trust it.

Who you are is not a problem to solve, but a gift to uncover.

And now that you've begun this discovery, your life becomes a conversation with God—a daily, continual unfolding of identity, purpose, and grace.

There will still be days when you forget who you are.

Days when old stories whisper louder than truth.

Days when comparison tugs, when fear rises, when insecurity knocks.

That's okay. Those moments don't erase anything. They simply invite you to return—to remember again what God has said.

Because identity is not a destination; it's a rhythm.

A returning.

A re-centering.

A coming home to the God who shaped you and the design He wove into your being.

As you leave these pages, my prayer for you is simple:

May you live lightly, because you're no longer fighting your own design.

May you live lovingly, because your gifts express God's heart.

May you live courageously, because your story has purpose.

May you live intentionally, because your design is needed.

May you live freely, because God delights in who you are.

And may you walk forward with this quiet, steady confidence:

You were created with purpose.

You are becoming who you've always been.

And the world will be brighter because you choose to live from your God-given design.

This journey is not ending here.

It's beginning.

Appendix A

Crafting Your Personal Design Discovery Declaration

Refer back to these pages for each puzzle piece:

Chapter 1: page 19

Chapter 2: page 26

Chapter 3: page 33

Chapter 4: page 39

Chapter 5: page 45

Chapter 6: page 52

Chapter 7: page 58

Chapter 8: page 64

Chapter 9: page 70

Chapter 10: page 76

Chapter 11: page 82

Chapter 12: page 89

Chapter 13: page 96

Chapter 14: page 102

Design Discovery Declaration Puzzle Pieces

1. ____

2. ____

3. ____

4. ____

5. ____

6. ____

7. ____

8. ____

9. ____

10. ____

11. ____

12. ____

13. ____

14. ____

Your Personal Design Discovery Declaration

Use the space below to write your own declaration.

About the Author

Cindy H. Carr began her faith journey on December 24, 1984. It didn't begin in a church service or with an altar call, but through a personal invitation from Jesus Christ while she was alone preparing for Christmas Eve. In that quiet moment, a relationship was born—one that transcended theology, tradition, and every expectation of what faith was "supposed" to be.

Over the decades that followed, Cindy immersed herself in theological study and served in both business and her community, yet her unwavering relationship with Jesus Christ has guided every step of her life and leadership. She has learned that love—steady, simple, and sincere—is the foundation strong enough to endure any storm.

In *God Made You, and He Doesn't Make Junk*, Cindy invites readers to discover the sacred truth of their identity. With compassion and clarity, she leads readers to quiet shame, silence lies and embrace God's intentional design. In a world of comparison and insecurity, she calls us back to the unwavering love that formed us on purpose.

www.ingramcontent.com/pod-product-compliance
Lightning Source LLC
LaVergne TN
LVHW011030110826
845149LV00015B/3369

* 9 7 8 1 9 7 1 1 9 2 0 2 4 *